KAYAK ROLLING

The Black Art Demystified

LOEL COLLINS

Photography by Franco Ferrero

Illustrations by Carol Davies

D1416911

FALCONGUIDES ®

GUILFORD, CONNECTICUT
HELENA, MONTANA

AN IMPRINT OF THE GLOBE PEQUOT PRESS

FALCONGUIDES®

Library of Congress Cataloging-in-Publication Data is available on file.
ISBN 978-0-7627-5082-5

Printed in China
10 9 8 7 6 5 4 3 2 1

Contents

Introduction. 5

How to Use This Book. 5
    How to Practice 5
    Flow Chart 6
    A Word About the Pawlata 8

HOW TO ROLL

1 Gaining Water Confidence 9
    1.1   Porpoiseing. 9
    1.2   Kayak Wrestling 10
    1.3   Crocodile Wrestling 11
    1.4   Roly-Poly. 12

2 Before You Roll. 13
    2.1   Capsize (Legs Out) 13
    2.2   Capsize (Knees Out) 14
    2.3   Capsize and Exit (No Spraydeck) 14
    2.4   Capsize and Exit (With Spraydeck) 16
    2.5   Swimmer Rescue 18

3 Learning to Roll—C to C as the Core 19
    3.1   Front to Back Action. 19
    3.2   Front to Side Action. 20
    3.3   C to C Action. 20
    3.4   Hands for Support 22
    3.5   Introduce the Paddle 23
    3.6   The Half Roll 23
    3.7   C to C Roll 24
    3.8   The Full Sequence 25

4 Learning to Roll—The Back Deck Roll 26
    4.1   Nailing the Hip Flick Poolside 28
    4.2   All the Way Around 30
    4.3   Partner's Hands 31
    4.4   Hands Supported by Paddle Loom. 32
    4.5   Using a Paddle 33

TROUBLESHOOTING

5 Head Problems. 34
    5.1   Go Back a Stage 34
    5.2   Revisit Water Confidence. 34
    5.3   Revisit C to C Body Actions. 35
    5.4   Eyes Open. 35
    5.5   Diving Mask or Goggles 35
    5.6   Blowing Bubbles 36
    5.7   Relax 36
    5.8   Swim the Boat to the Side. 37
    5.9   Use a Video Camera. 38
    5.10   Have a Break. 38

6 Body Problems (Hip and Waist) **39**
6.1 The Core (Land Drill) 39
6.2 Love Handles 40
6.3 Salsa Dancing... 41
6.4 Hula-Hula 42
6.5 The Trapeze 42

7 Body Problems (Various) **43**
7.1 C to C with Hand Support 43
7.2 Body Roll... 43
7.3 Nod Your Head 44
7.4 Nose Last 45
7.5 More Blowing Bubbles 45

8 Paddle Movement Problems. **46**
8.1 Finding the Surface 46
8.2 Feel for Resistance....................................... 47
8.3 Blade Angle.. 48
8.4 Top Arm 49
8.5 More Top Arm 50
8.6 Smelly Armpits... 51
8.7 Power Is Nothing Without Control 51
8.8 Fingertips 52
8.9 Dry Roll 53
8.10 Single Blade 54
8.11 Supported Practice....................................... 54

ROLLING FOR REAL

9 Preparing to Venture Out **56**
9.1 Finding the Set Up Points 56
9.2 Coping With the Unexpected 57
9.3 Feeling the Water 58
9.4 Submarines 59
9.5 Enders... 60
9.6 Make Your Own Rough Water 61
9.7 Specialist Kit... 62
9.8 Old Rope... 63
9.9 Creek Boats.. 64
9.10 Sea Kayaks 65

10 Rolling Outdoors. **66**
10.1 Cold Water 66
10.2 Head Game.. 66
10.3 Noise (Whitewater) 67
10.4 Moving Water (Whitewater) 68
10.5 Moving Water (Surf)...................................... 69
10.6 Soup and a Roll 69
10.7 Which Way to Roll?....................................... 70
10.8 Rolling in Turbulence 72

Conclusion **74**

Acknowledgments **75**

About the Author **77**

Introduction

I remember my first roll. It was on the River Tawe in South Wales. I actually pushed off the bottom but it was enough to make me realize that I could do it. That incident is living proof to me that the secret of rolling under pressure is mostly in the head. However I also remember my last swim . . . getting tumbled down a shallow creek in California and realizing that no one's roll is perfect.

For some the appeal of rolling is that it is perceived as the ultimate skill for the kayaker. For many people this is simply because they've had such a hard time trying to master the roll they are convinced that it must be the pinnacle of skill. The truth is that it is often possible to get people to roll very quickly if you push the right buttons, but that it then falls apart once you hit the cold water because the skill isn't "strong" enough. People become disillusioned and convinced it's some kind of "black art."

I wanted to write a simple book about how to learn to roll and how to deal with any little problems that may arise. Here it is!

How to Use This Book

This book is not very long and it would do no harm to read it all and familiarize yourself with all the exercises. Having done that, you can use the flow chart on the next page as a guide to choosing the right sequence of exercises for you. Be honest in your self-appraisal when using the flow chart.

All the exercises should be practiced on left and right alternately. This is essential if you are to develop a reliable, all conditions roll.

If you can already roll or have worked your way through the How to Roll section and are still having problems, move on to the Trouble Shooting section.

How to Practice

Quality practice is the key to good skill acquisition. So how do we make it count?

Skills have to be practiced and reinforced even after they have been acquired. Performing an exercise once isn't in itself proof that the skill has been learned. The exercise should be performed fluently, with the minimum of effort, and above all . . . consistently.

Some simple steps that will help to make your practice efficient are:
1. Warm up prior to any activity.
2. Ensure that you are physically comfortable in your boat.
3. Whenever you are practicing, work on both sides, alternately.
4. Initially, while you learn the basic technique, practice in blocks of time. Do the same exercise several times in the same "block," then rest.

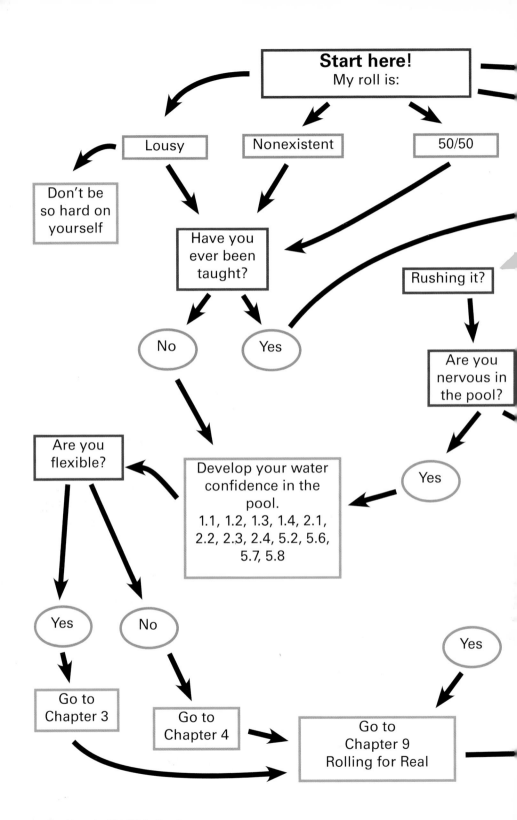

Start here!
My roll is:

Lousy

Nonexistent

50/50

Don't be so hard on yourself

Have you ever been taught?

Rushing it?

No

Yes

Are you nervous in the pool?

Are you flexible?

Develop your water confidence in the pool.
1.1, 1.2, 1.3, 1.4, 2.1, 2.2, 2.3, 2.4, 5.2, 5.6, 5.7, 5.8

Yes

Yes

No

Yes

Go to Chapter 3

Go to Chapter 4

Go to Chapter 9 Rolling for Real

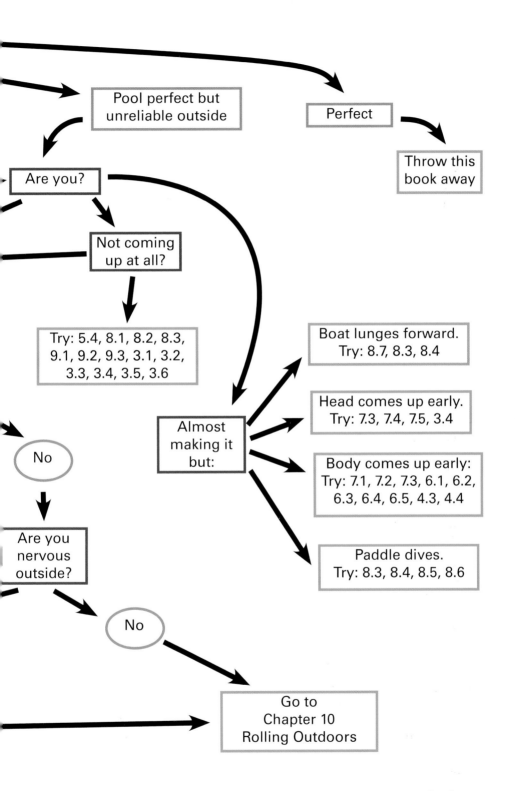

Pool perfect but unreliable outside

Perfect

Throw this book away

Are you?

Not coming up at all?

Try: 5.4, 8.1, 8.2, 8.3, 9.1, 9.2, 9.3, 3.1, 3.2, 3.3, 3.4, 3.5, 3.6

Almost making it but:

Boat lunges forward. Try: 8.7, 8.3, 8.4

Head comes up early. Try: 7.3, 7.4, 7.5, 3.4

Body comes up early: Try: 7.1, 7.2, 7.3, 6.1, 6.2, 6.3, 6.4, 6.5, 4.3, 4.4

Paddle dives. Try: 8.3, 8.4, 8.5, 8.6

No

Are you nervous outside?

No

Go to Chapter 10 Rolling Outdoors

5. Once you have the basic technique nailed, change things so as to vary the practice:
    - Different boats
    - Different paddles
    - Different parts of the pool
    - Have your helpers splash the surface of the pool
    - Start from a slightly different position
    - Start from the other side
    - Wear your buoyancy aid
    - Wear a helmet
    - Wear a cagoule
    - Try it with your eyes shut
    - Try it with your eyes open
6. After your session, warm down.

Remember: "Variety is the spice of practice."

—Martin Chester - Plas y Brenin coach

A Word About the Pawlata

I'm sure H.W. Pawlata was a nice fellow and, considering that he worked out the Pawlata roll after reading accounts of Eskimo rolls written by explorers, he did a great job. However, I'm not convinced he got it quite right. "Sacrilege!" I hear you shout. "He'll go straight to hell!" I hear you mutter.

In all seriousness, this book will not advocate the Pawlata or any form of extended paddle roll because it has little to offer the modern paddler. It doesn't work at all with low volume whitewater boats because the combination of massive leverage and the extremely laid-back body position causes the kayak to stern dip!

Even in a sea kayak it has severe limitations in that it takes so long to set up that in rough water you have at best a fifty-fifty chance of a successful roll. Even when you do come up you are holding the paddle in such a way that you can't use it as a paddle, which means that in rough water you'll probably capsize again.

Worst of all, it "grooves in" a body action and a reliance on brute force, which guarantees that, once paddlers have learned a Pawlata, they will find it very difficult to learn any other form of roll. *Therefore it should not even be used as part of a learning progression.*

Chapter 1 Gaining Water Confidence

Increasing access to swimming pools has made learning to roll easier. Rolling is not hard to learn but the sensations involved are unusual. Being upside down in the water adds an extra stress that often stops people from picking up this skill sooner. Water confidence is vital and the following exercises may help develop it.

1.1 Porpoiseing

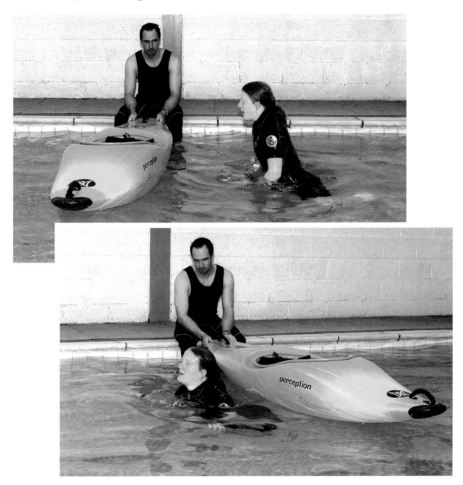

Get your partner to hold a kayak still and then swim under it. If there are a number of you, lay out a number of kayaks and swim under one and climb over the next or even swim under one, take a breath, and then swim under the next. It's fun and reminds us that having our head under water is no big deal.

1.2 Kayak Wrestling

Stand in the shallows facing your partner across a boat so that one of you is just in front of the cockpit and one of you is just behind. Reach across the boat and grab hold of the opposite edge. You then try and roll the kayak over towards you so that if you are winning your partner will be rolled over the boat and into the water on your side. Meanwhile your partner is trying to do the same to you.

1.3 Crocodile Wrestling

Climb onto the back deck of the boat and wrap your arms and legs around the boat. Now "wrestle" the boat over and over so that sometimes you are on top of the boat and sometimes you are under it. Great fun!

1.4 Roly-Poly

Hold your nose and squeeze so that your nostrils are closed and water can't get in. Now tuck into a ball and get your partner to roll you over and over an agreed number of times under the water. If you have had enough before the agreed number of rolls simply straighten out your body.

This exercise will habituate you to being disoriented under water.

Chapter 2 Before You Roll

Once you are happy in your boat, both upright and upside down, practice your capsize and exit. A confident capsize drill is important from a safety point of view and is important as a way of demonstrating confidence under water. If your capsize drill is rushed or panicky, you aren't ready to go on to rolling.

2.1 Capsize (Legs Out)

A good confidence builder is to capsize with your legs already out of the cockpit.

2.2 Capsize (Knees Out)

Take it a stage further now, legs in the cockpit but knees unbraced. You'll just fall out once the boat is upside down.

2.3 Capsize and Exit (No Spraydeck)

If you have never done a capsize drill before, practice it without a spraydeck first. As a precaution, make sure that your partner is standing in the water close by, ready to perform a "swimmer rescue" (see 2.5) should you get into difficulties.

1. Grip the boat by bracing your knees so that you don't fall out when upside down and capsize.
2. Wait till the boat is completely upside down (count to three if it helps).
3. Relax your knees, put your hands on the deck just behind your hips, and push the boat off your legs. (Do not lean back).
4. Come to the surface and get a hold of the boat.

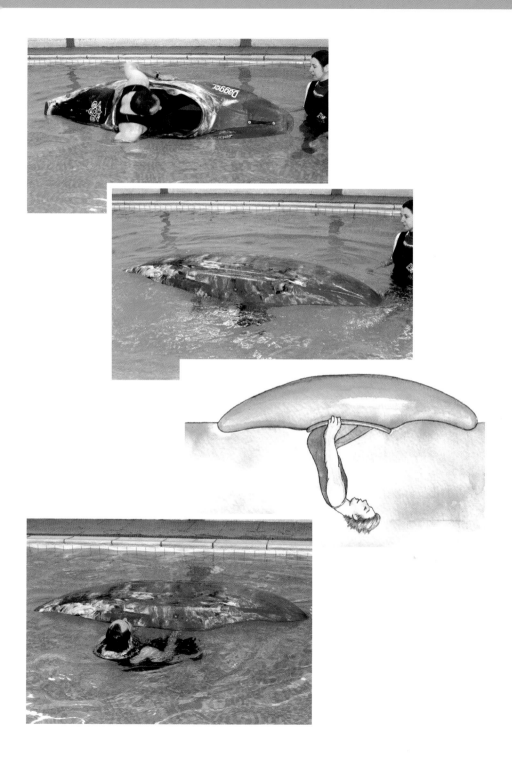

2.4 Capsize and Exit (With Spraydeck)

Once again, if this is your first time, make sure your partner is standing close by, ready to assist if necessary. As for 2.3 except that once the boat is upside down you have to use the quick-release strap to remove the spraydeck. You should practice removing the spraydeck a few times while you are still the right way up.

Use a nylon spraydeck until you are sure that you have got the hang of it as these will come off even if you forget to use the quick-release strap. Only once you are confident and practiced with a nylon spraydeck should you move on to a neoprene spraydeck.

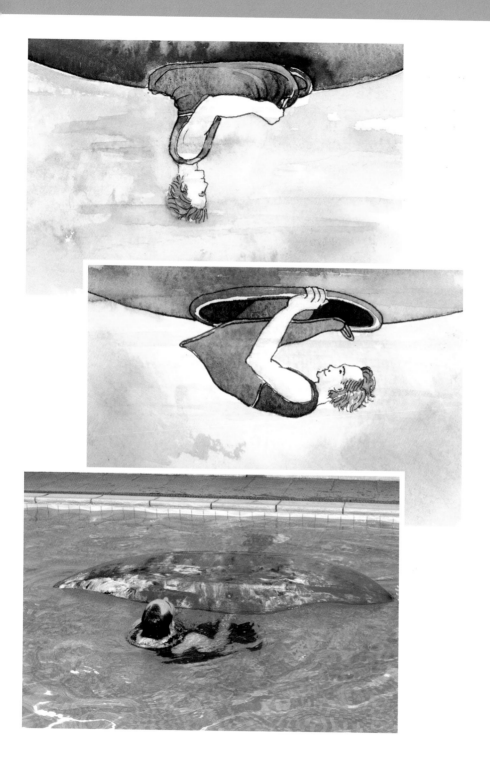

2.5 Swimmer Rescue

Now enlist the help of a couple of friends. Your partners will play a very important part in your rolling progression. With their assistance you can be rescued once you have capsized without leaving your boat and you can practice on both sides. When you've capsized and want to be recovered, simply bang on the bottom of your kayak. This is the signal for one of your partners to reach over your upturned kayak and grasp the cockpit rim. The rescuer keeps his or her arms straight and leans back. Providing you play your part by leaning forward, you can be recovered easily.

Chapter 3 Learning to Roll—C to C as the Core

Fundamental to any roll is flexibility in the lower back and hip, and a slow, controlled roll is more reliable in rough or whitewater. The C to C roll is by far the most reliable rough water roll. You should only consider learning the back deck roll if you lack flexibility in the waist.

The first stage is to develop confidence under water and an understanding of the range of movements required to perform the C to C roll. *Make sure you perform all these actions on both sides!*

3.1 Front to Back Action

Flip over, towards one of your partners, let the boat settle upside down for a moment. Let your body hang below the boat for a moment. Next, lean forwards reaching towards the bow of the boat with your hands. Then lean right back, sweeping your hands over your head and towards the back of the boat. When you've had enough, tap the boat so that you can be recovered.

3.2 Front to Side Action

Flip over and allow the boat to settle. Relax and let your body float below the boat. Lean forward with your hands extended forward, sweep your hands across the surface out to the right, then sweep them back to the bow. Then repeat the exercise to the left.

3.3 C to C Action

This builds on the previous exercise. Flip over in the same way. This time lean as far over to the left as you can, curving your spine sideways to do this and pushing your hands clear of the water. Next, slowly sweep your hands out and down towards the bottom of the pool and over to the right-hand side of the kayak. Use your spine throughout the movement, ending up with your hands out of the water on the right-hand side.

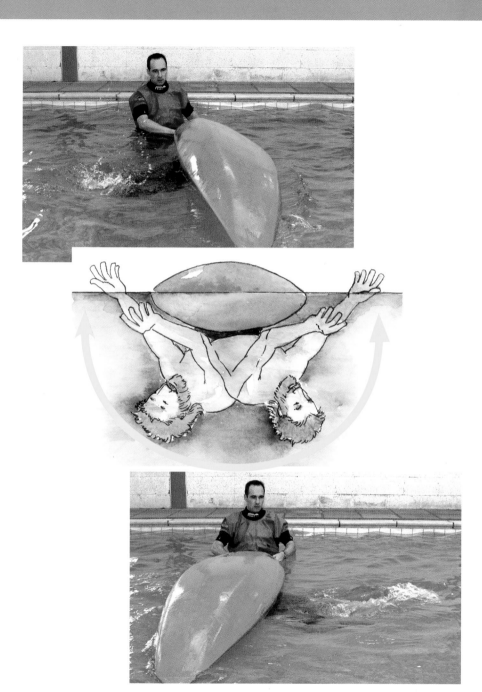

Once completed, tap the boat and get yourself recovered. Practice this exercise starting left and right so that you can do it on both sides.

This movement should be practiced slowly and deliberately.

3.4 Hands for Support

Flip over on one side. Reach up to the surface on the other side and have a partner support your hands. Get your partners to feed back to you how much weight they are supporting on a scale of 1 to 5. By concentrating on the use of the hip and waist action, aim to reduce this to a 1 on your scale.

3.5 Introduce the Paddle

Sit upright, holding your paddle horizontally in front of you. Have partner A gently hold the paddle blade that is on their side of the boat so that the paddle remains at right angles to the kayak throughout the exercise.

Let go of the paddle and capsize away from partner A. When upside down, reach up towards partner A and gently take hold of the paddle shaft. Roll the boat away from partner A, who will support the paddle blade, while partner B gently helps the boat upright if necessary.

3.6 The Half Roll

Repeat this on alternate sides until your partners no longer need to support the paddle blade. This is a half roll. Well done!

3.7 C to C Roll

The final step is to develop this into a full roll. Hold the paddle shaft in the normal way and then lean forward and place it in the water close alongside and parallel to the boat (the "set up"). Have a partner stand at the end of the kayak.

Capsize towards the paddle, let the boat settle, and allow the partner to move the paddle out to the starting point of the previous exercise. The partner can then tap the boat and you can roll up; again, do this alternating from side to side. Initially the partner may need to support the working blade but as your confidence increases the roll will develop.

3.8 The Full Sequence

Or . . . How it looks "for real."

Chapter 4 Learning to Roll—The Back Deck Roll

If you lack flexibility in the waist you may have more success if you develop a back deck roll. This lowers the center of gravity and makes your roll easier . . . on flat water. It produces a roll that is workable but not always reliable in very turbulent water.

If you've bought this book because your roll isn't reliable or you just can't seem to nail it, this is probably the roll you've been struggling with. If this is the case and you are reasonably flexible, work on the C to C roll. If flexibility is a problem, the back deck roll is your best option.

The key to this roll is a well timed hip flick.

Hip Flick!

4.1 Nailing the Hip Flick Poolside

Start at the side of the pool with your hands on the edge of the pool. Lean the boat over until your weight is supported by your hands and the boat is on its edge. Gently flex your hips so the boat flattens, lie back, and then push with your hands to bring your body over the back deck and then upright.

Gradually take the boat further and further over until you can recover yourself from being completely upside down. As you become more relaxed speed up the hip flick.

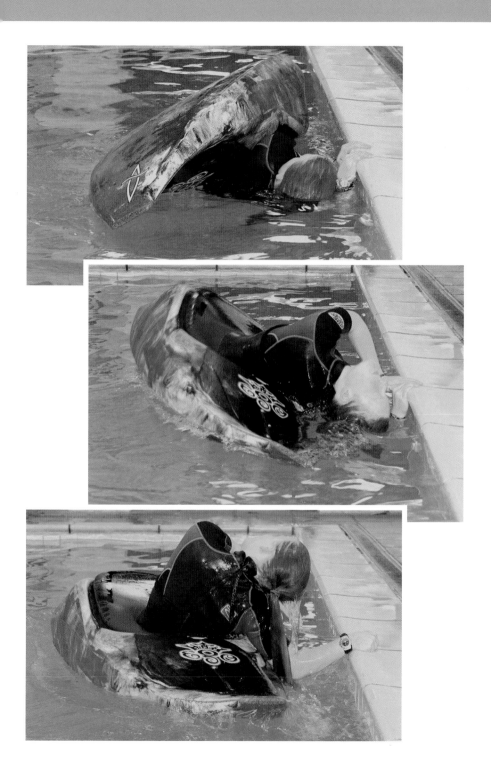

4.2 All the Way Around

Once you have mastered 4.1, capsize away from the edge so you can reach up and recover yourself having completed a full rotation.

4.3 Partner's Hands

Take a step back and move all these exercises into the middle of the pool using your partner's hand instead of the pool edge. Once the hip flick feels easy, progress on to using a paddle.

4.4 Hands Supported by Paddle Loom

As for 4.3, but repeat the exercises using a paddle loom held on the surface of the water by your partner for support.

4.5 Using a Paddle

The key here is the "set up" and a clear idea of what a back deck roll looks like. So find someone to show you a clear illustration of a roll (see pages 26–27).

Set up on the side opposite your partner by holding the paddle shaft in the normal way and then leaning forward and placing it in the water close alongside and parallel to the boat. Capsize keeping your paddle and body in the set up position. Let the boat settle upside down. Have your partner gently take hold of the paddle blade and

sweep it away from the boat on the surface of the water. As the paddle is moved, concentrate on flexing your hips as the paddle is swept out.

Repeat this exercise until the movement is second nature. Then you're rolling!

Troubleshooting

This section of the book deals with how to overcome particular problems in your rolling technique. These could be things you are doing wrong as a learner or worse still, bad habits that have become "grooved in." You will have to rely on your partners or an experienced coach to observe your performance and work out what the problem is. This section will give clues on how to spot the problems and possible solutions.

The problem areas are divided into the following sections:

Head Problems—Problems of confidence or orientation
Body Problems (Hip and Waist)—Problems with hip and waist actions
Body Problems (Various)—Problems with particular body actions
Paddle Movement Problems—Problems with the paddle action

Chapter 5 Head Problems

There are all sorts of psychological problems that you might run up against when learning to roll.

You might have problems gaining sufficient water confidence. Possible signs of this would be rushing an exercise to get it over with or repeatedly bringing your head up to the surface first when you know it should be last.

You might have problems with orientation under water. Possible signs would be being clear on what is required when upright and "losing the plot" when upside down. Your partners may observe that once upside down you move your paddle or body in the opposite direction to that which was intended.

A number of possible approaches and solutions follow.

5.1 Go Back a Stage

Orientation problems?

Sometimes people have problems learning to roll because they are progressing too quickly. This means that the foundations haven't set before they try to build on them. If you think this could be the case, go back a stage or two and practice until the techniques learned at that stage are "grooved in" properly.

5.2 Revisit Water Confidence

Water confidence an issue?

If you are showing signs of a lack of water confidence, revisit the exercises in Chapter 1.

5.3 Revisit C to C Body Actions

Water confidence or orientation issues

If water confidence or orientation under water is the problem, revisit exercises 3.1 and 3.2.

5.4 Eyes Open

Confused under water?

If you are upside down, under water, and have your eyes full of water, how could you make it more difficult to orientate yourself? You could shut your eyes!

Keep your eyes open under water. Your vision may be blurred but you will be able to see where the surface is and the silhouettes of your kayak and paddle. Practice swimming under water with your eyes open. Do the exercises in Chapter 2 with your eyes open.

5.5 Diving Mask or Goggles

Orientation

If you are still having problems with orientation, try using a diving mask for a while so that you can see clearly under water. It is important that you stop using the mask as soon as you can or you will become dependent on it.

5.6 Blowing Bubbles

Disorientated or distressed?

When learning to roll you can use a nose clip to prevent water going up your nose. However, if you become dependant on one you will eventually capsize and need to roll when you aren't wearing one, and your roll will probably fail. The secret is to blow gently out of your nostrils the whole time you are under water. This creates a positive pressure and stops the water getting in.

Practice by sticking your head under water and blowing bubbles by blowing air through your nose. Start by blowing quite hard then gradually reduce the pressure each time you practice. Keep doing this until you are blowing out through your nose so gently that you can keep your head under water for at least ten seconds . . . more than enough time to roll.

5.7 Relax

Tense and stiff?

Many people have problems rolling because they take a huge breath on capsizing. The effort of holding all that air in their lungs means that their muscles are tensed up.

Taking a more normal breath and blowing out through your nose will prevent this. Practice as for Exercise 5.6. You can even practice in the bath.

5.8 Swim the Boat to the Side

Need to learn to stay calm?

This is a good exercise that requires both orientation and self-discipline under water. Capsize and then, staying in your boat and keeping your head under water, swim your boat to the side and roll your boat using the pool edge for support. Start close to the side and gradually increase the distance you have to swim to reach the side of the pool.

5.9 Use a Video Camera

Can't visualize what you are doing?

A video camera is an incredibly powerful feedback tool. Get a partner to video your efforts. The ideal is to have one of those cameras with its own playback screen so that you get the feedback as soon after the action as possible.

It is also useful to review your efforts on a larger monitor while having a break from rolling.

5.10 Have a Break

Getting worse rather than better?

As you learn it is important to take it easy and stay relaxed. If your performance drops or you start to get frustrated take time out.

Let your progress dictate when you are ready to move on to the next stage.

Chapter 6 Body Problems (Hip and Waist)

The following exercise will help sort out any problems with your hip and waist actions.

6.1 The Core (Land Drill)

Don't really have a feel for the C to C action?

This is a good bank-based exercise with which to develop hip flexion and an upright body posture.

Sit at the foot of a wall with your bottom at the base of the wall and your back against the wall. You should feel your "sit bones" in your bottom on the floor. Keeping the pressure equal on both "sit bones" reach your hands over and onto the floor on your right-hand side. Gently "walk" your hands away from you without lifting either buttock off the floor.

When your hands can't go any further, lift the opposite buttock off the floor.

From this position recover yourself by moving the leg and hip back without putting weight on your hands. If you're getting it right your hands will slide across the floor effortlessly.

Got it? Good. Now try the other side!

6.2 Love Handles

Hip and waist flexibility and control

The key to any roll is good hip flexibility and range of movement. In your boat simply lift your knees alternately so that the boat rocks from side to side but your body stays above the boat. Do it slowly and gracefully from side to side. You know you're getting it right if you can feel it in your love handles (the excess flesh that even the skinniest people have above their hips)!

6.3 Salsa Dancing

Hip and waist flexibility and control

Side to side is only the half of it. Forwards, backwards, round and round. It all develops a range of movement. Imagine you're line dancing at first but aim for the Salsa.

6.4 Hula-Hula

Hip and waist flexibility and control

Once your hips are loosening up, progress to the Hula-Hula. Try moving your hips in a set pattern. While sitting in your boat, push your hips forward, return to center, backwards, return to center, left, return to center, and right, return to center. Then vary the patterns . . . any sequence will do.

Imagine shapes. Draw squares with your hips. Circles clockwise and counter-clockwise. How about triangles?

6.5 The Trapeze

Hip and waist flexibility and control

If your pool allows it, set up a trapeze at chest height. Try all the balance exercises holding the trapeze as if it's a paddle and try to do them without putting weight on the ropes.

Chapter 7 Body Problems (Various)

The following exercise will help sort out any problems with other aspects of your body action.

7.1 C to C with Hand Support

Does it feel as if your arms are doing all the work?

Go back to Exercise 3.4.

7.2 Body Roll

Still working too hard with your arms?

Go back to Exercise 3.4. This time, instead of one of your partners helping you finish the righting movement by supporting your hands, get them to support your body a little, so that your arms aren't involved.

7.3 Nod Your Head

Is your roll failing because your head comes up first?

At the point your roll is stopping and you sink back beneath the "waves," nod your head back towards the water. It will help with your hip flex.

7.4 Nose Last

Can't avoid jerking your head up at the last second?

As you come up, turn your face so that you look at the water as you finish the roll. A good indicator is if the water runs off your nose as your face leaves the water.

7.5 More Blowing Bubbles

Can't avoid the tendency to bring your head up early?

Blow bubbles as you roll. Turn your face so that you blow bubbles as long as you can during the roll.

Chapter 8 Paddle Movement Problems

The following exercise will help sort out any problems with aspects of your paddle movement.

8.1 Finding the Surface

Paddle dives during the sweep?

Is your paddle diving into the water as it's swept out during the roll? This can be due to not actually finding the surface with the paddle, at the very start of the sweep. A good exercise is to pause once the boat has settled upside down and then push the paddle from the water and tap the surface a couple of times before starting the sweep out to the side.

8.2 Feel for Resistance

Sometimes a subtle paddle movement will tell you everything, so *gently* pull on the paddle to check that there is some resistance. This resistance will tell you that the blade is "square" to the water.

I sometimes make a little cross with the loom—up, down, left, right—to confirm that I've got resistance.

8.3 Blade Angle

Paddles dives during the sweep?

If the paddle dives during the sweep it is often due to the angle of the blade at the start of the sweep. Have someone gently turn the blade to the angle for the sweep. Too little and it will dive, too much and it will act as a sweep stroke and turn the boat.

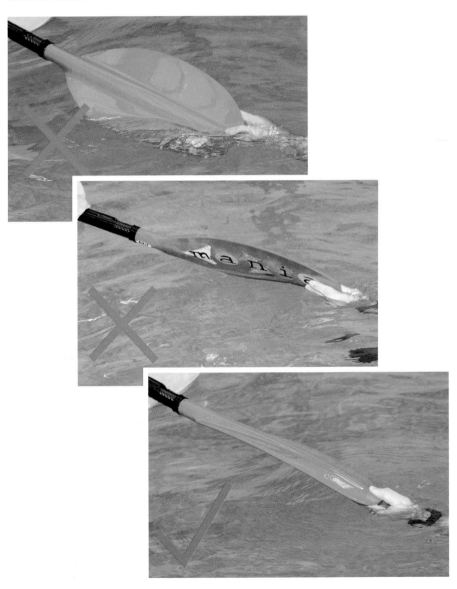

8.4 Top Arm

Is your top arm reaching for the sky?

The blade can be driven deep if the upper arm (the one closest to the underside of the boat) is pushed up during the roll. The giveaway is the straight arm above the head and the paddle at a near vertical angle.

Focus on having the arm bent with the hand close to its shoulder.

8.5 More Top Arm

Is your sweep finishing at the back of the boat rather than out to the side?

This happens when the upper arm is pushed forward and straightened out during the roll. It will put the paddle in a position where it provides little support and your body is in a weak position for a C to C action.

The paddle can also dive during the latter part of the sweep because the wrist is also straight. This unfeathers the blade causing the blade to twist up, decreasing the surface area available to the water and decreasing the support available.

As with 8.3, focus on having the arm bent with the hand close to its shoulder.

8.6 Smelly Armpits

Still having problems with 8.4 or 8.5?

This upper arm is crucial. If the movement is difficult to coordinate, find another job for it! Put a tennis ball in your armpit and roll without losing it. It keeps the arm down and close.

8.7 Power Is Nothing Without Control

Is your boat shooting forward?

If your boat is accelerating off forward you are probably not sweeping out and are simply powering up on a monster forward stroke. As well as taking a good deal of effort this is a very unreliable form of roll in that it relies on perfect timing. A simple solution is to tape a swimming float to your paddle.

8.8 Fingertips

Still using brute force? Try holding the paddle with your fingertips. You will have to be gentle and you will develop control.

8.9 Dry Roll

Still having problems with 8.7?

Try taking your boat out of the pool and doing half rolls on dry land . . . your paddle will have to sweep out!

8.10 Single Blade

Still having problems with blade angle?

Try using a canoe paddle to roll with. The T grip helps make you more aware of exactly how much blade angle you are using.

8.11 Supported Practice

Moving the paddle in the wrong direction?

Get "set up." This time capsize away from your paddle but get a partner to support your body so that although the boat is upside down your head is still on the surface. In this position, practice the paddle movement.

Stage 1: Make sure the paddle is on the surface.

Stage 2: Sweep it out to the side until it is at right angles to the kayak.

You can get your partner to support your body with one hand and use the other hand to guide your paddle.

Chapter 9 Preparing to Venture Out

Once you have developed a reasonable "pool" roll, the next step is to spend time in the pool simulating the more challenging conditions you may meet outdoors.

9.1 Finding the Set Up Points

When you capsize for real it is unlikely that you will be set up to roll. It is important to be able to find the set up position when you are under water.

While still upright, practice finding the "set up" position. Close your eyes and memorize how it feels. Make sure you are aware of three key points in your set up. It could be where you contact the boat . . . it could be the amount of bend in your arm.

Once you are happy doing it upright, try repeating the exercise upside down.

9.2 Coping With the Unexpected

Capsize with your paddle in a variety of positions other than the set up position and then find the set up position while under water. Keep your eyes open; at least you'll know where the surface is!

Try capsizing with your paddle over your head. Try capsizing while forward paddling. Try capsizing mid-drawstroke. How about while paddling backwards?

9.3 Feeling the Water

If you can do this you will develop a truly "bomb-proof" roll. Repeat the exercises in 9.2, but instead of "setting up," go straight to a position where your paddle is on the surface at right angles to your kayak . . . and roll up.

When you move onto moving water, this will allow you to react to and exploit the power of the water. If you become disoriented, you can always tuck back into the set up position.

9.4 Submarines

Take your deck off and let your boat fill with water. Now try rolling as the boat sinks! This changes the way your boat behaves. It introduces an element of unpredictability, which forces you to adapt and change your body actions and paddle techniques to suit.

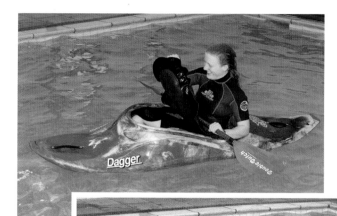

You'll need airbags in the stern for this exercise.

9.5 Enders

Get used to the chaos of whitewater or surf. Allow your partner to tip the boat, end over end, from the side of the pool.

9.6 Make Your Own Rough Water

Get a partner to hold onto the stern of your boat and lift it up and down as you roll. Further sensations of chaotic water can be added by getting other helpers to splash the surface of the water around you.

9.7 Specialist Kit

If you are going to wear a buoyancy aid and helmet, get used to rolling with them on in the pool.

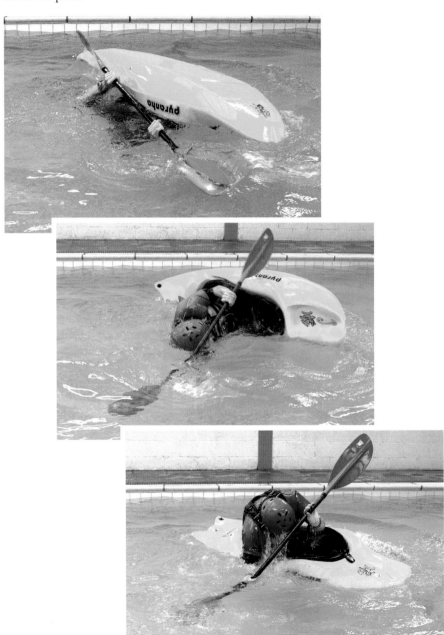

9.8 Old Rope

The sensation of moving water can be recreated in the pool by using your friends to  pull the boat up and down the pool as you practice your roll. You will find it much easier to roll on the "downstream" side so it is just as well that you have been practicing on both sides throughout!

9.9 Creek Boats

Many pools have rules that only allow you to use the "pool" boats provided. If you promise to clean your boat thoroughly, inside and out, the pool manager may agree to let you bring your own boat in.

Creek boats are easy to roll but the creek isn't easy to roll in! It's best to develop a "quick and dirty" roll that protects your head and body. The body is better protected if you adapt the C to C so that you come up leaning forward rather than over the side.

9.10 Sea Kayaks

If you'll be paddling a sea kayak outside, try to use one in the pool. Sea kayaks are no harder to roll but the timing is different.

Do everything at a more leisurely pace and give the boat time to capsize completely before you reach for the surface. If you use the back deck roll, think of the hip flick as more of a hip rotation.

When you learn to roll a sea kayak outdoors, lose the deck cargo! By keeping deck clutter to a minimum you make rolling or deep water rescues a lot easier.

10 Rolling Outdoors

Rolling outdoors can feel like a big step. The techniques are the same but the environment, unlike in the pool, is changeable and unpredictable. A number of exercises and tricks to help you get over this hurdle follow.

10.1 Cold Water

Cold water will take your breath away. This can be unnerving but is a normal response, so don't worry. To overcome this, splash your face and the back of your neck with cold water prior to practicing outdoors on flat water. If the nerves of the face and a sensitive nerve on the back of your neck get used to the cold, the response can be reduced.

10.2 Head Game

Up till now, when you have capsized, the correct and instinctive thing to do has been to get out of the upturned kayak. You now have to do the complete opposite and hang on in there while you sort out your roll.

This is primarily a "head" problem. You have to convince yourself that you really do want to stay in your boat. Motivation is the key. Men often hang on in there because they don't want to "lose face" in front of their friends. Women are far more sensible and usually have to convince themselves that rolling is the safer and more comfortable option.

10.3 Noise (Whitewater)

The other unusual thing in moving water is the noise. As you progress your rolling onto moving water, try it out in an eddy at the bottom of a drop. It'll be noisy and a bit cold but safe.

10.4 Moving Water (Whitewater)

Whitewater moves, but don't let that faze you. Initially, practice your whitewater roll in the gentle shoot at the bottom of the rapid. It'll be cold and noisy but the trick is simply to relax and count to five; this will allow the paddle to flow naturally to the side. By the time you get to five, the boat will be moving at the same speed as the water and the roll will be as easy as on flat water!

As your confidence builds you can move into faster water and still count to five. As you become more attuned to the whitewater environment you will be able to react to it and roll more quickly.

10.5 Moving Water (Surf)

When you capsize in surf and you haven't yet developed a good moving water roll, one trick is to wait until everything stops moving and roll in the trough between the waves before the next wave breaks over you! As you become more attuned to the surf you will be able to roll sooner.

10.6 Soup and a Roll

In surf, try a few rolls in the "soup," the smaller broken waves close to the beach. You can get used to the movement of the water in the safety of the shallows, and even get a partner to guide/support your paddle blade. Make sure your partner is on the seaward side and that you are between him and the beach. This is mainly for your partner's safety, as the incoming waves will push your boat away from your partner rather than towards him or her. It will also ensure that you will be helped rather than hindered by the movement of the water (see 10.7).

A kayak surfer will often feel the moving water pushing on the blade of the paddle and roll up without needing to go to a set up position. The ultimate version of this is rolling while still on the face of the wave.

10.7 Which Way to Roll?

On flat water, or if you time your roll as in 10.4 and 10.5, it doesn't matter which way you roll. However, if you want to roll quickly and reliably in moving water, you must go with the flow. If you go with it rather than fighting it, moving water can make it easier to roll!

Almost all the previous exercises in this book have prepared you for this in that they involve you capsizing on one side and coming up on the other so that the boat rotates through 360°. You should also have been practicing by capsizing to the right and left alternately.

In whitewater you usually "catch an edge" and capsize upstream. If you go with the flow you will roll up on the downstream side and the force of the current will assist the rotation of the boat and support your paddle.

In surf you usually capsize away from the face of the wave (towards the beach). By rolling up towards the face of the wave you gain support from the movement of the water within the wave itself.

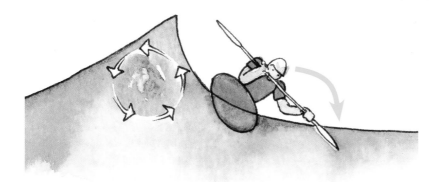

Either way . . . the trick is to go with the flow.

10.8 Rolling in Turbulence

The pool is a great place to learn. The controlled environment enables you to pick up the techniques involved in rolling. The skill of rolling is something different!

The photos you see are a sequence of one roll of fourteen done on a cold February day. Each roll was different and none of them could be described as "textbook." In turbulent water the environment is constantly changing so your choice of techniques and timing will differ each time. This ability to select and adapt is what makes your roll skillful. The following tips will help:

- If there is no chance of hitting a rock, count to three before you roll. The boat will then be moving at the same speed as the water, making the roll simpler.
- Run through the roll in your mind before you practice it. Make sure the image is clear and accurate.
- Don't expect to do a "textbook roll." There is no such thing when it boils down to it.
- A good reliable roll is like a recipe. The ingredients need to be right but the seasoning you will add to taste. The building blocks need to be there but you must tune your roll to suit the tastes of the water!